"In a world that so often feels gne
soothing balm for the soul."

> – Charlie Edwards,
> Lightcoder, Weaver & Cosmic Healer
> charlieedwards.me

"Jo's words call you back to a deep remembering of our
connection to the water. Inspiring you to lovingly and
compassionately remember you."

> – Yolandi Boshoff,
> Spiritual Coach
> divinesoul.me

"Wild Currents is elemental, primal, raw, fierce and
delicious. It is like a hug from Mother Earth herself, or one
of Jo's "salty kisses". It will move you to tears and laughter,
and bring you back to all that truly matters in one quick dip.
It is pure, magical, deep-reaching medicine for the soul."

> – Zoë K. M. Foster,
> Embodied Expression Artist &
> SacredExpression™ Facilitator

"Reading Wild Currents took me on a full-body experience that stirred the watery eddies of my soul. There is something rather special about an author that truly writes from the heart; baring it so that the world can benefit from the medicine that lies within this sacred and deeply personal space. Jo writes with such a profound and moving purity that invites genuine connection – a connection that will stay with me long after closing the pages of this beautiful book."

– Em Mulholland,
Shamanic Practitioner & Word Doula
@one_spiritual_mother

wild
currents

POEMS ON THE
TRANSFORMATIVE POWER OF
WATER IN TURBULENT TIMES

JO GIFFORD

Image credits:
Artwork by Zoe Foster, p. 15, 63, 74
Photography by Miles O'Carroll p. 0, 8, 67
Photography by Yasmin Finch p. 29, 79, 50
Photography by Becky Wright Brand Photography p. 95

Paperback 978-1-913590-50-5
Ebook 978-1-913590-51-2

The Unbound Press
www.theunboundpress.com

Hey unbound one!

Welcome to this magical book brought to you by The Unbound Press.

At The Unbound Press we believe that when women write freely from the fullest expression of who they are, it can't help but activate a feeling of deep connection and transformation in others. When we come together, we become more and we're changing the world, one book at a time!

This book has been carefully crafted by both the author and publisher with the intention of inspiring you to move ever more deeply into who you truly are.

We hope that this book helps you to connect with your Unbound Self and that you feel called to pass it on to others who want to live a more fully expressed life.

With much love,
Nicola Humber

Founder of The Unbound Press
www.theunboundpress.com

CONTENTS

You may journey through waterfalls, rapids, floods, stagnation, strong undercurrents, and the sheer terror of drowning, at times.
But the magic is in the moments.
It's the glimmering diamonds of light that dance off the waves.
It's the flow and the ease that comes after the flood.
It's the depth, not the surface.

Foreword

It's August 2021, and I am beginning the journey of writing *Wild Currents*, this book that has made itself known to me over the last few months.

She has been tapping me on the shoulder, in the way that books do, letting me know she wants to be shared.

Right now, we're still figuring out how to live in a nearly post-pandemic world.

Over the last 18 months, all of our lives have been turned upside down.

Everything as we knew it changed in an instant, and we have all, collectively, been through profound change in one way or another.

The thing that helped me the most during this most crazy of times, much to my own surprise, has been finding solace in the wildly sacred, healing magic of water.

I'm far from alone in this.

Wild swimming has exploded over the last year. Groups are popping up all over the place, and our stories of how we found strength, resilience, community, and healing through water have taken the media and the mainstream by storm.

My own story alone has been carried by the BBC, The Telegraph, Spirit and Destiny magazine and Top Santé magazine, and a story I wrote on Medium blew up as I explained how water and cold water swimming helped to heal me after the death of my dad in the cruelest of times in the harshest of circumstances.

I know that my story represents something that is happening across the country and across the globe.

I see it in my own community; as the co-founder of the Cambridgeshire & Peterborough BlueTits, our group grew enormously in just a few months.

I know how much finding the magic of water means to people.
I know how much this is spreading.

And so does this book.

Wild Currents appeared to me at a time when, to be honest, I didn't want to be writing another book.

The exhaustion and the fatigue of dealing with grief, having lost several family members and friends through the pandemic, meant that my body and my system just didn't feel ready to write again – certainly not something as long form as a book.

But the more people I met, the more stories I would hear, and the more my own story would capture something for other people.

I knew this was something that had arrived for me to do.

So, here I am, saying a sacred yes with joy, with the understanding that whenever we embark on a journey like this we never know where it might take us.

Goodness knows I never knew that stripping naked for a swim on that first day would take me to where it has done so far; from meeting amazing people, to swimming the longest distance I ever have, discovering how the cold heals, meeting new friends, mentors, soulmates, and having the opportunity to share the love and the magic of the water with not only my own friends and family, but people far and wide.

It's a real honour and a pleasure to be able to bring my words, my stories, and some stories of others who also love this healing element to you all.

In all honesty, I hold some guilt in being a newbie to this incredible activity and writing about it.

I recognise that so many incredible people already know of the magic of water and have done for a long time.

So, let's name that here.

I am not an expert. I am not claiming to have discovered wild swimming – it just arrived in my life when I needed it.

Maybe it has for you, too.

Maybe water has been calling you, and you don't know why.

Through this journey, I have discovered just how lovely the swimming community is; how kind, welcoming, friendly, creative, inclusive and warm they are.

So, I am daring to speak up, knowing that I am one voice among many, trusting that my words reach whoever they need to.

Welcome to the world of wild swimming, cold water, misty mornings, warm onesies, colourful bobble hats, hot chocolates in flasks, laughter in the waves and magic in the soul.

It is my hope that *Wild Currents* meets you where you need it.

I hope that this book that you hold in your hands sparks something in you; whether it's the magic of the cold and how the cold helps us find resilience, or the simplicity of the fact that water is always all around us and we need a reminder to use it to embrace it, to engage with it and immerse in it.

Or maybe it's the reminder that when we feel locked down we can find freedom, whether it's in the foggiest river on the coldest day, or with our toes in the sea, watching the waves ripple over our feet.

Maybe it will spark some creativity within you, to respond to the water with words, imagery, or a form of expression that feels right to you.

Water connects us to all that is.

Water has its own sacred geometry and vibration, it has long been associated with purification of our bodies, minds and spirits, and it's an essential part of our world.

So, here is my humble offering to you, dear reader.

The stories and vignettes here are offered as mini experiences in themselves.

They are mainly poems, short stories, observations that arrived in my mind and my soul.

Many have been shared on social media, and I know from the way they have been received that they offer a certain magic in their essence.

As you dip into these pages, find the words when you need them.

They often arrived for me fully formed, sometimes in enormous waves, sometimes in trickles.

It is my honour and my deepest pleasure to connect us through these words, through this element right now.

So thank you, dear wild one.

So much love,

Jo

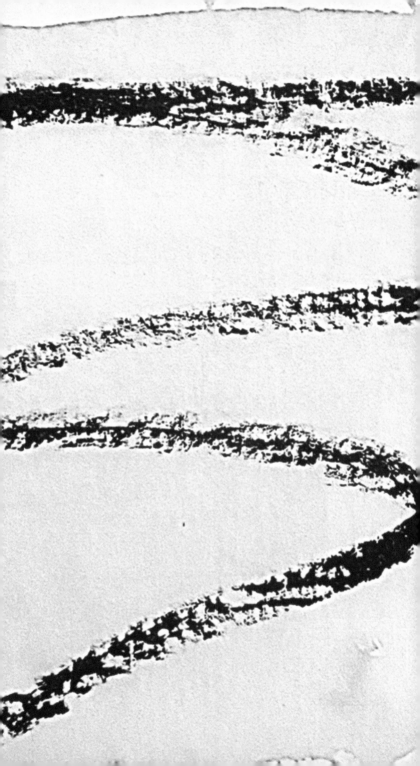

Re-Wilding: My Story

I hated swimming. I couldn't stand being cold.

So, to end 2020 as a fully signed up cold water swimming addict was as much of a surprise to me as to anyone else.

So, how did I end up taking the icy plunge, and – more importantly – why on earth would anyone anywhere *near* their right mind want to?

Well, I lost my mind a bit in 2020, and the magic of the water saved me.

I suddenly found myself being one of those smiling girls on Instagram in a bobble hat, advocating the self-torture of cold water swimming – and it's the best thing that could have happened to me.

Earlier in 2020 my world as I knew it had started to fall apart, as had all of ours, in this transformational, chaotic year.

With the backdrop of Lockdown 1.0, my dad died.

My lovely Papa had suffered from dementia for a couple of years since having a second stroke, and he passed away from COVID-19 in May.

A casualty of the care home system during the time a virus is rampaging the world, and a really vulnerable frame that was a shadow of himself, we said goodbye, via FaceTime.

Losing a loved one is devastating enough.

Losing a loved one when you can't be with them, when you have to say goodbye via an iPad to your hero, when you can't hold their hand, is a whole other level of cruelty.

Grief came in waves, crashing over me with a numb bewilderment.

My partner had also been made redundant.

Home schooling was happening.

Some other huge personal shifts were taking place.

In short, things were a hot mess.

By early June I was an anxious heap; a human accumulation of panic attacks, tears and exhaustion, steeped in rum and clutching a bottle of Diazepam.

During days when I just didn't know how to get through each moment, walking in the fields behind our house had been a daily practice.

The simple act of putting one foot in front of the other seemed so symbolic, so certain – often the only thing I knew to be true that day – and I felt held by nature as each day unfolded.

Poem from June 2020

The fields outside my house are the keepers of my range of raw emotions.

Over the last 3 months they have been where my tears fall, where my heart opens, where I howl into the rain.

It's where I walk barefoot on the grass, where I tell the trees my pain, grief and loss, and whisper my fears in the boughs of their ancient wisdom.

It's where the lakes absorb my salty sadness, the light reflects love and vibrates with my vision, and the cherry blossom tells me of a fragrant hope.

They are where I share my open and broken heart, where I feel my humanity burning, hot in my veins, dream the treasure maps of my future, and breathe in the oxygen of now.

Walking the same paths on different days in different states, I see the paradox of growth and transformation.

Nothing changes.

But everything.

Some days feel peaceful, expansive, promising.

Some days are tumultuous, visceral, raw, my knees buckling with pain on the gravel track.

Some are hollow. Some are happy.

Some days have all the human in every moment.

Some seem to glide, unscathed, while others leave scars.

And all the while the leaves on the trees bud and unfurl, the grass finds its height until walking through the dew feels like rain.

The wheat emerges from the ground and reaches for the sky, and the sole, red poppy stands bright and alone in her temporary glory.

Transformation is everything and nothing.

All the things and none.

It's rapid expansion, whole love, and deep loss.

It's moments, lifetimes, seconds.

It's the spaces between the heartbeats, the silence between the breaths.

It's me. It's you.

It's us. It's here and it's now.

It's cells, soul, soil and surrender.

And I keep walking.

Connected.

I am sure I am not the only one to have re-discovered the beauty of where they live during lockdown.

Being part of All That Is seemed to be so crucial during those months.

I sat in the tree I had adopted as my favourite one. I cried. I meditated. I had long walks.

The lakes in the nature reserve shimmered and felt like a soothing soul balm, a sanctuary to sit near.

I began to crave the water. To be near it felt like a physical need.

I live pretty much on the river.

I am from this area, and had never felt the call to water so strongly as in 2020.

In the summer, I started walking to the river and taking a dip.

I first went entirely naked, in a secluded spot by some fields close to my home.

In a time when freedom felt so compromised, when the whole world felt constricted, dangerous, controlled – there was such freedom in re-wilding.

The water seemed to clear my head. All the fogginess and grief of the day felt washed away.

I felt lighter, refreshed, free.

sanctuary

I loved having my feet on the earth, toes in the mud, sliding into the water and letting it hold me.

Something new had awakened within me.

I started paddle boarding on a local lake.

I needed the water, the space, the nature, the air, the oxygen.

I needed the healing water magic.

I hadn't thought beyond summer for swimming; I knew I would miss the water and usually I often struggle in winter with the lack of daylight and ability to unbox my day due to hibernation.

So, when a couple of fellow local wild swimmers reached out to me to be a wild swim buddy throughout the cold months, I was excited to give it a go.
At the same time, a dear friend of mine, Lisa Monger, had started a group of BlueTits Chill Swimmers in Leigh-on-Sea, and I was seeing a social media feed full of smiling women splashing about in the ocean.

I was inspired, excited and intrigued to see if the magic would still work in the cold.

On October 31st I had my first cold swim, in the sea at Chalkwell Beach, with Lisa holding my hand.

As the waves crashed over me and I yelled with joy and freezing cold elation, I let the sea wash away the anxiety, depression and profoundly human experience of the year.

I stood with my feet in the sand, my toes grounded, soaking up the energy of the beach and of autumnal nature, and I sobbed into Lisa.

Apparently it's not unusual to experience a raw, elemental release in the cold water. It doesn't surprise me, either.

There is something so primal, so wild, so natural about letting the cold heal us that it seems to all make sense (albeit a cold, shivery sense).

After my first cold dip I felt elated, I felt alive, euphoric, clear-headed and vital.

I was hooked.

The next day I had my first cold river dunk with my new wild swimming buddy, Yasmin.

We immersed ourselves in the River Great Ouse. I was ecstatic to have discovered the magical euphoria I had heard about from other cold swimmers, and excited to find a spot to do it locally, and someone to do it with.

At the same time, a friend from my gym also reached out to swim, and suggested we form a local BlueTits Chill Swimmers group – the Cambridgeshire BlueTits.

Within just a couple of weeks, Elise and I had 100 members in the group, we had been interviewed on BBC Radio Cambridgeshire, and we had discovered many more people locally who wanted to take a cold, wild, dip and dunk.

I have a few chronic illnesses – endometriosis, chronic fatigue, fibromyalgia – that I thrive with, but whose presence is often known in my life.

I began to feel an energy and elation after each dip, but also pain relief.

My healing journey from these conditions has been long, complex and varied, and this extra piece of the jigsaw puzzle was a new one for me.
The benefits of cold water immersion are well documented – from reducing inflammation, helping with depression, staving off dementia and increasing our immune systems to many more.

For me, it's all these and more.

It's the soul food of a waterside chat and a sense of achievement with every dip.

It's knowing I can endure stress and come out elated.

It's testing my body and my mind.

It's finding like-minded humans.

It's the pure joy of being part of nature – walking on a riverbed on a foggy morning with my breath turning to mist and raindrops falling onto the water from the trees is a pretty spectacular experience.

So, how does it feel?

For my first river swim in November the water was 10 degrees. Since then, I have dipped in 4.5-degree water with an air temp of -1.

When you first get in, it really is an assault on the system.

The whole body focusses, and every sense is acutely heightened – after all, the body registering being put into immediate danger does sharpen every nerve.

Breathing with intention at this point is essential (as is yelping, as I often do).

It's like a sharp focus combined with an immediate hug.

A freezing cold body of water activates the parasympathetic nervous system pretty quickly, and it's like accessing a state of meditation.

I stay in for as long as feels appropriate; it changes day by day depending on how I feel, the water temperature, air temperature, where I am in my monthly cycle, how tired I am, and what I feel able to endure.

Sometimes I dip for just a few minutes, sometimes I stay in for 10-15, or longer.

Afterwards I feel AMAZING.

I feel invigorated, yes, but also connected, clear, alive, fully present, and surprisingly warm....

...until the after-drop kicks in.

Learning to get dressed and keep heat in while my body is still dropping in temperature has been fun.

I favour a Dryrobe and a onesie with layers of thermals to make the whole thing as quick and easy as possible (the bag lady look has become a staple, and a quick way to recognise fellow cold water swimmers at a glance).

I learned the hard way that neoprene socks and gloves are game changers as the temperature drops; crying in pain as my feet rewarmed from blocks of ice taught me that one.

So, what has cold water swimming given me?

It has given me a way to connect with nature, to feel acutely alive, and to experience freedom during lockdown and a pandemic.

It has given me resiliency, bravery, confidence, a new community of like-minded humans.

It has given me human connection; connection to myself, my body and my emotions, and a huge appreciation for the nature on my doorstep.

That first swim was like a gateway drug to more confidence, more adventure, more seeking, more community, more ways to get on and in the water.

I have my sights set on all kinds of places to strip off and freeze myself in.

Often, I feel an increased anxiety as I drive to the water, as though my body knows it's about to have a primal, sacral release.

Knowing I have a place and space to process embodied emotions feels really important to me right now.

Grief and stress took me to the water to re-wild, but people find cold swimming for all kinds of reasons – dealing with mental health, stress, depression, life changes – or just 2020.

So that's part of my story, and it continues to unfold, ebbing and flowing with the currents and the streams of life.

Jo.

Introduction

Welcome to the world of wild swimming and open water.

This is where souls are restored, heavy hearts are healed, and the deep immersion in nature is resourcing a new age of seekers.

All around the world, hundreds of thousands of people are finding swimming for all kinds of reasons – dealing with mental health, stress, depression, life changes – or just the times we live in.

Now, "swimming" may mean dipping, swimbling, paddling, splashing about in water, or a longer swim. It doesn't matter. Just being in the water is what I mean when I use that word.

It's no wonder wild swimming and cold water swimming exploded in 2020; what we have all been processing is just beyond all comprehension.

But we have nature. We have water.

We ride the currents, and go with the flow.

My story of how wild swimming saved me from heartbreak, grief and chronic pain has been hitting the news, the headlines, and striking a chord with thousands of fellow wild swimmers who have also taken the plunge.

The explosion of wild swimming during the pandemic is testament to the power of water, how nature is plugging us back into source, and how the need to immerse in nature is a powerful tool for change.

We are all embracing what the ancients knew, what our souls remembered, and what science is now proving – water is essential to our wellbeing.

We all have our own stories of how water came to be the healer, the space holder, the friend, the wild craving in our lives.

For me it was grief, stress, and anxiety.

2020 in a nutshell.

What I discovered when meeting other wild ones is that we all take our pain to the water.

Mental, physical, spiritual, emotional, existential, cellular pain, we let the cold, the current – the raw, visceral, elemental power – hold us.

Within that place of solace, that simple, sacred place of healing, we find a reconnection to ourselves; to resilience, to nature, to who we are as human beings.

All that from getting in the river or the sea?

Well, yes – and I am here to share my story and some stories of others who have ridden the waves of the wildest currents with the magic of water.

Deep loss, heartbreak, depression, stagnation, the edges of human experience – all transformed through a relationship with water.

Dip in, take a swimble with the words, and float with them as you need.

Let them hold you.

Swimming belonged to the lithe, strong-shouldered, fearless kids with floppy, chlorine-bleached hair, the ones who would dive to the bottom of the deep end, way past that slope that filled me with dread.

Swimming belonged to the "sporty kids", not the arty, academic, curvy and self-conscious me, who avoided the pool and its intensity of sound, chemicals and terrifying vulnerability at every possible moment.

Swimming never felt like a world in which I belonged.

It seemed like an overly loud, overwhelming busy place, with posters depicting all the things you cannot do here – belly flopping, running, petting – spring into my memory; the air thick with the shrill, raspy notes of children laughing, the lifeguard's whistle, and the deeply terrifying sound of people diving into the end of the pool that was reserved for my nightmares.

But the sea?

The sea felt playful, inviting, wild and wondrous.

I loved the salt in my hair, bodyboarding the waves, and floating between the sky and the horizon, willing the moment to stay.

It took me a long time to realise that the magic of the water

wild

and

wondrous

is mine to immerse in, anytime.

I didn't seek out lakes, crave the river ways from my home county, or plan adventures that would replenish and reconnect me.

It was never in my awareness.

Maybe I was never ready for it to be until it was time.

And now it's time.

It's time for me, and for hundreds of thousands of others who are daring to dip, who are being drawn to the water in a way we never knew was possible, shedding old stories, misconceptions and identities that didn't quite fit, removing them carefully like we unzip a wetsuit and step aside.

Those stories may have kept us safe, but they also kept us protected from a wildness, a magic that's ours to reclaim.

So, whether we dip, swim, swimble, dunk or just float, reclaiming space in the water and redefining what it means to us is a ferocious, powerfully potent act of love.

We witness changes in the seasons, the quality of the air, the water, the skies when we visit the water.

From frosty, foggy mornings with breath folding in shapes

above the ripples, to low, transparent water with
the riverbed in view, each change is subtle,
tangible, and an anchor to the here and now.

Hold me.

Help me have the
courage to float.

Rock me, gently, with
your elemental power.

Show me how to flow, to
ebb, to be

With the wildest of
currents,

A human body of water.

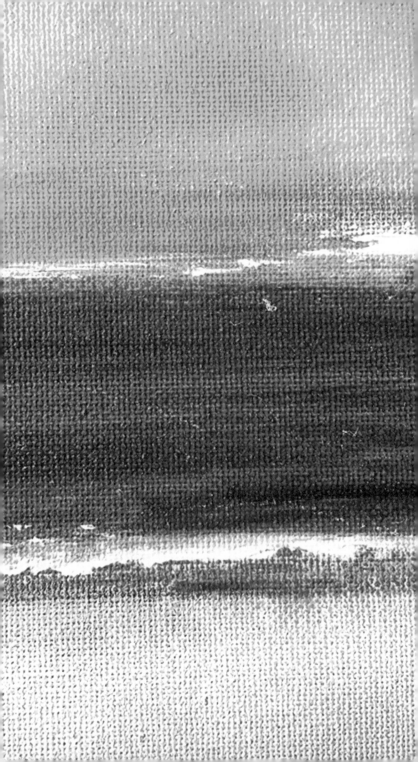

A salty, tidal kiss.

Wash the day from my feet, my bones, my veins.

Fill me with dust of ancient rocks and stars

Suspended;

The cycle of rising and falling

From Earth to the heavens

Made real.

In your element.

While the lily pads dance

The light waves ripple.

A fluid mirror of earth in the skies,

Clouds that embrace the water before it falls.

Embodied, re-imagined

Flowing through the riverbank in rainbows.

I wander with a wildness.

I seek

At the seam of the seasons

The birdsong stitches time

Where wildness calls in ripples

The dandelion's ghost still floats

Like clockwork

To the river

Suddenly you realise that you are so used to stripping off by a riverbank, running to the sea, or sneaking a swimsuit into your backpack on a bike ride just in case there is a chance or a dip.

Something courageous happens when we rewild and make the water our home.

This is a legacy I am honoured to be leaving my daughters – to show them, to teach them that our bodies are amazing just as they are, and that when you are immersed in the blue magic of water, the gratitude and presence you feel for that experience far outweighs worries about self-image.

Life is here, now.

Water gives us the courage to feel it, to live it, and to love the sandy, muddy grit of it all while we do.

life is
here, now

When I think of grief, and feel the way she ebbs and flows – sometimes a calm undercurrent, barely noticeable, yet still moving, sometimes a salty tidal wave – water as a healer makes so much sense in my cells.

The very cells that are also made up of water, in the body that sheds salty tears like the ocean, sometimes a gentle stream of a memory that makes my eyes mist up, sometimes a howl that reaches the edge of the horizon.

Whatever emotion we bring to the water, it teaches us so much.

An icy fog will turn back into a balmy day, where once there was a burst bank and floods, there will be shallower depths to paddle in.

Water welcomes it all.
It becomes us, we are (literally) in our element.

Water knows.
She has cycles too, and promises that raindrops turn into waves on a beach that nibble your toes and ask you to float, joyous and carefree in the salt and the sun.

From the hollow comes the halcyon.

water

knows

In the water, we are not our insecurities, our lists of faults we have been trained to apologise for, our wobbly bits, wrinkles, or age.

We are not a target weight, a work in progress, a before, an after, a socially acceptable size, shape, or set of macros in flesh and bone.

In the water we are present.

We are infinite.

We are here, now, then and thereafter.

We are reminded to take up space as wide and as far as the ocean, knowing that sometimes even the vastness of the sea needs to find moments of calm in the trickle of a stream or the divine isolation of a raindrop.

In the water we remember that we are part of all that is, all that was, and all that is coming.

We are stardust, ancient atoms and molecules made human for this moment in time; we are washed with the same essence that has cleansed and purified for millions of years.

The water holds us within and without.

From riptide to raindrop and all in between.

The water holds us in wisdom, and reminds us that we matter.

That we ARE the matter, that we are made of the same element that ranges from ferocious power to quiet, gentle fog.

Suspend your fears and your worries in the waves, the ripples and the flow of the H2O that reminds us, refines us, rewires us, and requires us to just be here, now, whole.

I hugged you as the sky melted,

Blurring dusky, salty light.

Colour pouring onto the waves

As they swayed with the sunset rhythm

Of an August Sunday.

The day fades,

I hold your smile in my throat.

The ocean is wide,

The tide and time keep moving

And I let you go.

Longing for you to always swim home,

To where I will always be,

A love with no horizon.

an endless
sea of love

"Catch a wave with me,"

Holding my hand,

The ocean goes up your nose.

We laugh into the blue.

"Here's the next one!"

Joy is salty on our smiles,

Here, now, pressing pause.

I remember you on this stretch of sand,

Your tiny legs paddling in the shallows,

Your toddler fist in the palm of your dad,

Splashing in the foam in the distance.

Grown now, my inner child and yours

Playing, precious, knowing

You are growing, going,

Making your own waves,

Taking my heart with you,

An endless sea of love.

The reclamation of salt water on her skin;
An act of self-love, and a long, painful journey of undoing.
The layers of her very being wept,
Sores, welts and tears
As the topical steroid withdrawal left her body, mind and soul.
Shedding, revealing,
peeling her trauma in layers.
Unbinding the prison of her skin.
She longed for the water.
She longed to feel the cold, wild element around her,
A hug of rawness, bathed in hope.
Slowly, she regained herself, her strength, and her fire.
She waited for the day she could step into the sea without pain.
For the moment when the salt kissed her wounds,
The ocean whispered
"You made it home."

For Zoë, with wild love.

the

reclamation

of salt water

on her skin

100 swims of healing

Frail, scared, and vulnerable, the residents were first in
line.
When the virus hit our care homes, they were gone,
ghosts in their place, shadows roaming the halls.
A storm raged in her throat.
The waves of scorching, salty grief ran down her
cheeks in silent resignation.
She carried on, drowning inside.

Their lives were put in boxes.
Day after day they left, a life gone without a trace,
departed in pain, in fear, and lonely among a sea of
faces in masks whose eyes they did not recognise.

Anxiety swallowed her whole, sucked into a hurricane,
and blew her across an unknown landscape, breathless,
terrified, and silenced.

She took her pain within.
Her neural pathways embodied and embedded the
anguish.
She mourned for the faces she would no longer see,

The devastation on their hearts was palpable, painful like a bed sore of emotion.
The water held her close.
Taking the plunge was her solace, her safe place, her turning point of recovery.

The 100 swims of healing have cleansed her wounds and turned the tide of the trauma.
The care homes and their humans will never be forgotten.
Holding the hands of the dying, taking the place of families held apart by tragedy is always within her soul.

100 swims are healing her.
Each wave shapes her, moulding her gently back to wholeness.

The tears became the ocean.

For Rachael, with wild love.

Palms on the pebbles in her pocket, she waded into the deep.

They don't tell you about the pain of living sober.

The black hole inside could drown her, even if the water didn't.

She just wanted it to end.

She longed, deep in the place where her heart used to thrive, that the blackening, sharply rusted loss of herself to be swallowed by the sea.

Up to her shoulders in the ocean, eyes on the horizon, she changed her mind.

Trembling, weeping, afraid. Cold.

From the core of her being, so close to the end, the tears came.

She cried, letting the ocean hold her tears, her fears, the tiniest wave of a new beginning.

As light as gossamer, a promise of strength began to weave itself into her soul.

One yoga pose led to another, then another, then another.

She began to run, jumping in the sea to cool off, to revive, to feel alive.

Her body was renewing, slowly, slowly, slowly. Each sinew finding oxygen where the darkness had left only shadow.

The very ocean that nearly took her last breath became where she found more life.

From one groyne to the next she swam, then the next, then the next. Onwards.

Her strength was moulded, shaped, refined by the sea.

The woman who went out to wade to her death
Found new life in the water that kept her afloat.

She became a warrior, moving the energy in her body on the shore, taking it out to the waves.

New life flooded into the place it nearly left her.

The tide knows her secret.

It also became her strength.

For Jules, with wild warrior love.

Her body bore the tales of her pain.

Weighed down by life,

Wading through the days,

Swallowed by the ache of existing,

She lost herself,

Joy was buried deep in her bones.

Her joints cracked, aching;

Embodied sadness filled the spaces where her spark
was just a shadow.

They wanted her to have surgery,

To change her body, to mend and repair the
brokenness.

But the sea became her medicine.

Paddling, then swimming, then fully immersed,

She changed her cells with the elements.

Rebuilding, re-wiring, re-finding herself wave after
wave.

Deep torment, taken out by the tide,

Alchemised to ecstasy.

Her love of life takes others out into the ocean,

The ripple effect of soul deep healing

Made possible with a step into the sea.

For Kathleen, with wild love.

celebrate
your
edges

You are invisible over 40.
You have wrinkles to smooth,
A belly to lose,
And don't mention your hormones,
We don't want to hear.
Keep your anxiety and your pain hidden.
Work harder, longer, more.
Try to look younger.
Do, do, do.
You aren't enough yet.
Who are you to love yourself?

The sea says:
Wild goddess, your power grows every day.
Take a moment to be in the sea
Breathe in deep, just be.
Your body matters.
You have wisdom,
Scars that map out your life,
You live in full colour, full range;
Celebrate your edges,
Revel in your essence,
You are wondrous as you are.
Feel, breathe, be, be.
You are already enough.
Who are you?
Love yourself.

The wild water falls.

Just for now, I stand.

My feet on the pebbles,

Rooted in the flow,

Then I am gone.

A shadow, glimpsing time.

The water moves,

Icy, powerful.

Slicing through seasons,

Washing through rocks

Standing still after the mist of me

Returns to raindrops.

His mind was a maze.

Anxiety ravaged his waking moments,

Waterlogged trauma dwelt in his cells, his soul, his spirit.

Discharged from service, he fell into a marshy swamp of darkness;

Lost, lonely, terrified,

Disconnected.

Word of the wild man reached him.

Could the breath and the cold really change a life?

The things he had seen would haunt his waking life and the worlds beyond sleep.

With nothing to lose but himself,

He began to explore.

The cold, so present, sharp, and all-consuming

Reconnected his body and mind.

Present, he used breath, the very force of life,

To explore a new path, a new way of being.

Being is what mattered most.

Before he could begin to live again,

To be, to find space to exist without pain

Daily dips and the presence of cold

Nurtured him back to living,

The freezing depths reaching a light

Still glowing beneath the ice of trauma.

Braving the cold every day,

He raised money for the homeless,

Discovering a purpose beyond the battle within.

The breath, the cold and the water brought him home.

For Bryan, with wild love.

He breathed in courage,
One misty, painful lungful at a time.
Breath by breath,
Inhale, exhale.
He began the mountainous climb to repair his cells,
Back from the brink, a new hope ahead.
As he lifted the weights,
The weight fell off.
Slowly, surely, one workout after another
He was shaping this body of a warrior in recovery,
Remembering an inner fire,
A strength that's a visceral flame,
A drive to find this awakened power.
When his mind raged and the demons awoke,
He moved his body,
A relentless war against the dark.
Then the water.
He found a way to deal, to heal,
To feel connected, human, possible.
The water soothed the battle in his brain,
It became a balm for a body and mind
Reconnecting to soul.
The waves and the sea flooded into the cracks,
Clearing out pain, a salty salve for anxiety,
He rises, like the ocean.

For Dave, with wild love. x

Leaves of burnt umber,
Licks of warm light.
Smiling into September,
The air edged with mist.
Cradled by the promise of cold,
Floating in the liminal.
The edges of Autumn ripple.

When anxiety coils

The water calls.

A diamond-lit deep,

Shifting, shedding, shaping

—

Holding the moment in a

cold gasp of now.

The river holds the light.

The swirling sea foam where I wiggled my toes

Becomes the steaming steep of my Earl Grey brew.

It rolls into tears down my cheeks,

And holds the howls I cry into the deep.

It becomes the hot bath in which I soak,

Skin red and prickly in the bubbly, scented mist.

It's the rain trickling onto my nose as I am drenched in the storm,

The sharp cold splash, gasping in the river,

Hugging me close in the flow.

It's the cycle of water

Taking her shape

Saturating our senses,

Witnessed always. The water knows.

witnessed
always

We float.

A dusky dip,

Leaving midlife in the mud

For a moment,

Laughter hanging in mist

Above the foggy October flow.

Dip your toe,

Find a shallow to step in the flow

Let the cold bite

Feel the light

On your face,

Your shoulders,

Your soul.

Swallowed whole,

Heart held by raindrops,

Satiated, drenched,

Remade.

Both the container
And the contained.
Shifting, shaping,
Shapeless, forming,
Becoming, shedding
Remembering.
Reclaiming,
Wholly wild.

wholly
wild

happy
in your skin

Isn't it obscene

To be seen,

Naked by the shore,

Or shaking as you change

By the lake in the rain?

Or is it freeing,

A sense of just being,

Wholly alive as you shiver,

Drenched in the coldness of the river.

Happy in your skin,

As you begin

To feel more like you,

Than ever before.

So we go back for more...

I cup a warm mug of coffee in my hands, holding it against my face, bringing my cheeks back to life, although the smile is already radiating, shining with a light that's a different kind of warmth.

I am buried under a duvet, fluffy socks on my feet, wrapped up in thermals, my onesie and my hat.

My skin is still tingling from the cold, turquoise water. My limbs are still finding their blood flow, pulsing with the presence that comes from cold immersion in the salty water under a mist of autumn rain.

This, right now, is happiness.

Fresh bread, peanut butter, hot coffee and the glow from the morning's salty, cold wake up call.

When you meet the sun in the coldest rivers
Knowing that the shivers make you feel
Alive, present, brave.

Who are you becoming?
Chasing the waves,
Letting salty, icy water melt your fears.
Raw, feral, wild.

What have you discovered?
Finding your soul recovers in ripples,
That you float into resilience,
Powerfully in your brilliance.

Pain has been my teacher for a very long time.

Chronic, searing, savage,

It has shaped me like glass in the ocean

For 25 years.

Thrown around in the waves,

Smoothed from a sharp, rigid fragment.

My soul knows that the scars have made me,

But the human me, thriving, growing, hurting,

Finds humble relief in the water.

The cold numbs the edges

Where the jagged aches still sting

And in the bright light, cold rivers and the salty sea

For a moment again I am whole, just me.

The roaring sea and a faint
autumn mist share the
essence of water as their
soulmate.

From hot tears of grief to
gentle beads of sweat, you
are both powerful and
gentle at once.

An ocean of possibility
floods within you.

Stepping into a cold, liquid sky

A swell of inverted heavens
The mirage reflection displaced by my feet.
Droplets of winter in flux,
Numb limbs await.
Alivening, awakened,
Immersed in a palette
Of painterly presence dispersed.

this

is

all

Frost on the earth, a moorhen for company, and heavy

skies soaked with November rain ready to fall.

This is all.

Walking into winter with heart, soul, lungs and limbs

ready to enfold the cold as it seeps into the soil, the air,

and the river.

Where the cold bites

Soaking bones, seeping into shadows
Pinching presence with a ghostly exhale.
Nowness in my toes, my fingers,
My heart
Beating, drifting, shifting.
A vapour trail of sighs.

The world is fractious
Tired, disbelieving, divided.
Grief reignites,
My heart heavy, swollen,
Exhausted, empty.
I stand by the riverbank,
Barefoot on the icy grass,
Stepping slowly into the flow.
The water can take my weight,
The cold holds my sadness
When the freezing river burns,
I gasp, a voice rasping
From a depth inside
Jolted to the present,
A gift;
An icy reminder I am alive
That water still flows
My body remembers.
We did this before.
When the temperature drops
We adapt.
When deep sadness floods,
We float.
When the cold river holds me
I am alive.

A frosty, star-spun mist

Tide as teardrops

Hung among the cobweb jewels.

Where the swan glides,

I hide.

Nature's spa rippling,

My breath as steam,

High above the river,

Carrying my voice to the ocean.

Today I found you in the water.

Just a glimpse,

You caught my eye.

A beam

Lit beneath a bough

Drenched with sunlight,

An orange pink promise;

Possibility, reflected deeply

In the mist of today.

Tomorrow's flood.

Acknowledgments

There are so many people to acknowledge who helped to bring *Wild Currents* to life, and I'm so grateful for each and every one of you.

First and foremost, to my darling family, and my incredible partner Miles. Always steadfast and unwavering in his patience, for the last few years he has been documenting my swims, encouraging me all the way, and patiently waiting by the side of rivers, lakes and seas while I go and splash about with joy on my face.

My daughters, who have found the courage to do their own wild swimming, and for whom I'm so excited that the magic and joys of enjoying the outdoors have also lit their spirits up. Being in the water with you, Eva and Mia, brings me joy (and makes me cry a bit, which makes you laugh).

To my dear Yasmin, who I'm so honoured to have swum with through two winters now, and whose partnership and dear friendship exploring wildness in our River Sessions is something I hold so dear. The River Sessions are soul therapy, and a part of my week I treasure.

My darling Elise, who was brave enough to start the Cambridgeshire BlueTits with me, whose mermaid soul and joyful spirit I am so grateful to know. Thank you for your boundless energy, support, and love.

To everyone in our Cambridgeshire and Peterborough BlueTits group that's now grown to such an incredible community; as we pass the baton on to Joyce and Sarah it's a pleasure to watch the group grow more and more. Each and every one of you is incredible, and it's been a joy to be part of the story of it.

To Sian and the team at BlueTits HQ – thank you for all that you do, for your vision for the community, and the wonderful way you do it.

To my dear Lisa Monger, who took me from my very first ever sea swim and who passed on the magic of cold water to me with such love, and a hug that I will remember forever.

To Nicola at The Unbound Press, who has once again held space for this book to come through as she needs to, with all the love, support and unboundness from this gorgeous family of authors.

To my dear Zoë Foster, who created my bespoke wild power painting that has been so instrumental in birthing this new book and stepping into my wild creatrix energy, and also for your love and friendship as I have gone through this journey.

To all the journalists and media who have held my story so far – sharing how wild swimming has enabled me to cope with grief, anxiety and loss in a profoundly difficult time has meant that my story can reach the hearts of many others.

To those whose stories I have shared in this little connection of vignettes, I am so grateful; it's been an honour to witness your stories and to hold space for them in this way. Thank you for your courage and bravery. I hope I did you proud.

And finally, for everyone who has read my poems or shared my words; you have been instrumental in helping me realise that my words do hit people where they need them – right in the heart.

And finally, for you, dear reader who has this book in your hands. Thank you for being part of my journey too by reading this book, by embracing the words that I've shared here.

You are part of my journey too, and I do hope the words meet you when you need them most.

Jo

About me

I am an author, writer, creative thinker, wild swimmer, and prolific human connector.

I love and lead with language and fully expressed living as my legacy, and believe in Writing Wild as a way to process the experience of life.

Come and connect with me over on Instagram on @wildcurrents and @thejogifford, or email jo@jogifford.co with your takeaways from this l'il book.

CPSIA information can be obtained
at www.ICGtesting.com
Printed in the USA
LVHW070410120722
723217LV00001B/1